Mel Bay Presents

The Christmas

Carols Arranged
for Acoustic Guitar

by Elias Barreiro

Visit us on the Web at www.melbay.com — E-mail us at email@melbay.com

Contents

Angels We Have Heard On High

Arranged by Elias Barreiro

Traditional Latin

Allegretto maestoso

Going To Bethlehem
(Vamos a Belén)

Arranged by Elias Barreiro

Traditional Chilean

Andante con moto

The First Nowell

Arranged by Elias Barreiro

Traditional English

Coventry Carol

Arranged by Elias Barreiro

Traditional English

Andante sostenuto

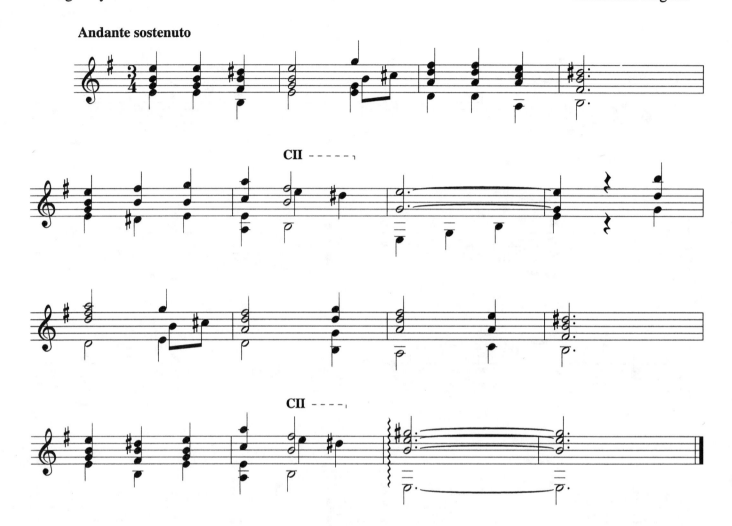

Cántico

Arranged by Elias Barreiro

Traditional Venezuelan

Silent Night, Holy Night
(Stille Nacht, Heilige Nacht)

Arranged by Elias Barreiro

Franz X. Gruber
(1787-1863)

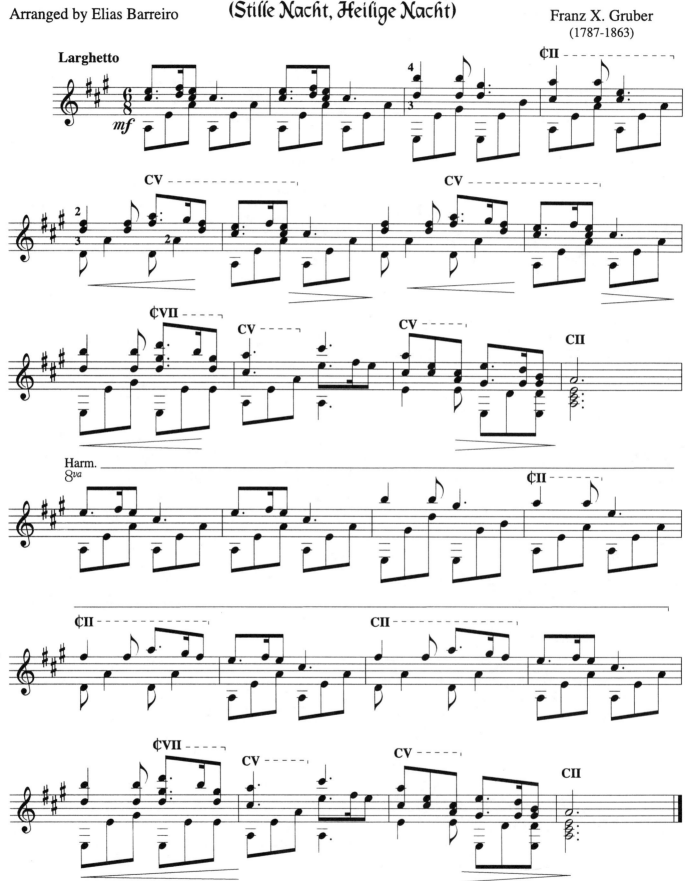

O Come, All Ye Faithful
(Adestes Fideles)

Arranged by Elias Barreiro

Traditional Latin

Andante moderato

9

The Three Ships

Arranged by Elias Barreiro

Traditional English

Moderato

O Bethlehem
(Oi Betlehem)

Arranged by Elias Barreiro

Traditional Spanish (Vizcaya)

O Christmas Tree
(O Tannenbaum)

Arranged by Elias Barreiro

Traditional German

Good Christian Men, Rejoice

Arranged by Elias Barreiro

Traditional German

Hark! The Herald Angels Sing

Arranged by Elias Barreiro

Felix Mendelssonn
(1809-1847)

The Holy Child
(El Santo Niño)

Arranged by Elias Barreiro

Traditional Puerto Rican

Andante sostenuto

Masters in this Hall

Arranged by Elias Barreiro

Traditional French

Allegretto moderato

Good King Wenceslas

Arranged by Elias Barreiro

Traditional English

Jingle Bells

Arranged by Elias Barreiro

James Pierpont
(1822-1893)

Cantemos, Cantemos

Arranged by Elias Barreiro

Traditional Venezuelan

The Seven Joys of Mary

Arranged by Elias Barreiro

Traditional English

Allegretto con moto

What Child Is This?
(Greensleeves)

Arranged by Elias Barreiro

Traditional English

O Little Town of Bethlehem

Arranged by Elias Barreiro

Lewis H. Redner
(1831-1908)

Deck the Halls

Arranged by Elias Barreiro

Traditional Welsh

The Twelve Days of Christmas

Arranged by Elias Barreiro

Traditional English

Precioso Querube

Arranged by Elias Barreiro

Traditional Venezuelan

We Wish You a Merry Christmas

Arranged by Elias Barreiro

Traditional English

Allegro con brio

Jolly Old St. Nicholas

Arranged by Elias Barreiro

Traditional American

Allegretto con moto

Away in a Manger

Arranged by Elias Barreiro

Traditional German
(Attributed to Martin Luther-1530)

Away in a Manger

Arranged by Elias Barreiro

Traditional English

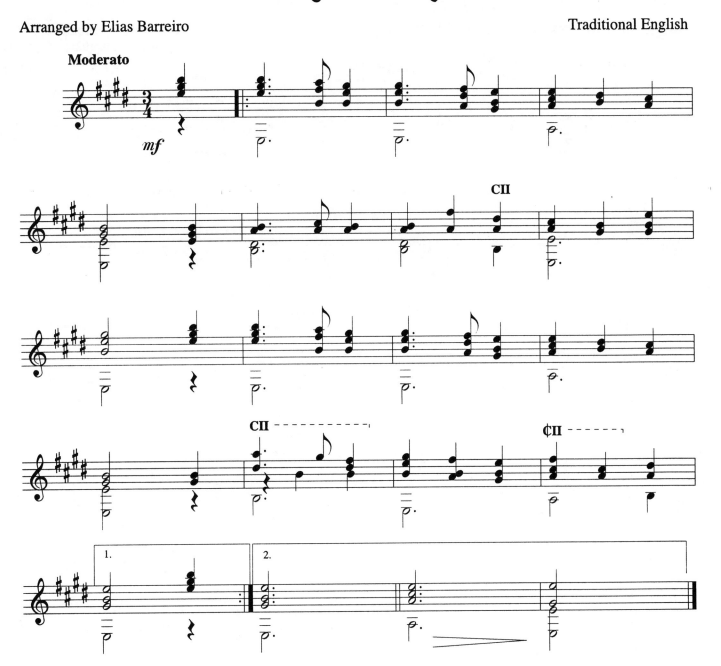

Away in a Manger

Arranged by Elias Barreiro

William J. Kirkpatrick
(USA 1838-1921)

Away in a Manger

Arranged by Elias Barreiro

Traditional Basque

Joy to the World

Arranged by Elias Barreiro

George F. Handel
(1685-1759)

It Came Upon a Midnight Clear

Arranged by Elias Barreiro

Richard S. Willis
(1829-1900)

poco rit.

I Saw Three Ships

Arranged by Elias Barreiro

Traditional English

We Three Kings of Orient Are

Arranged by Elias Barreiro

John H. Hopkins
(1820-1891)

God Rest You Merry, Gentlemen

Arranged by Elias Barreiro

Traditional English

O Sanctissima

Arranged by Elias Barreiro

Traditional Sicilian

Angels We Have Heard On High

Arranged by Elias Barreiro

Traditional Latin

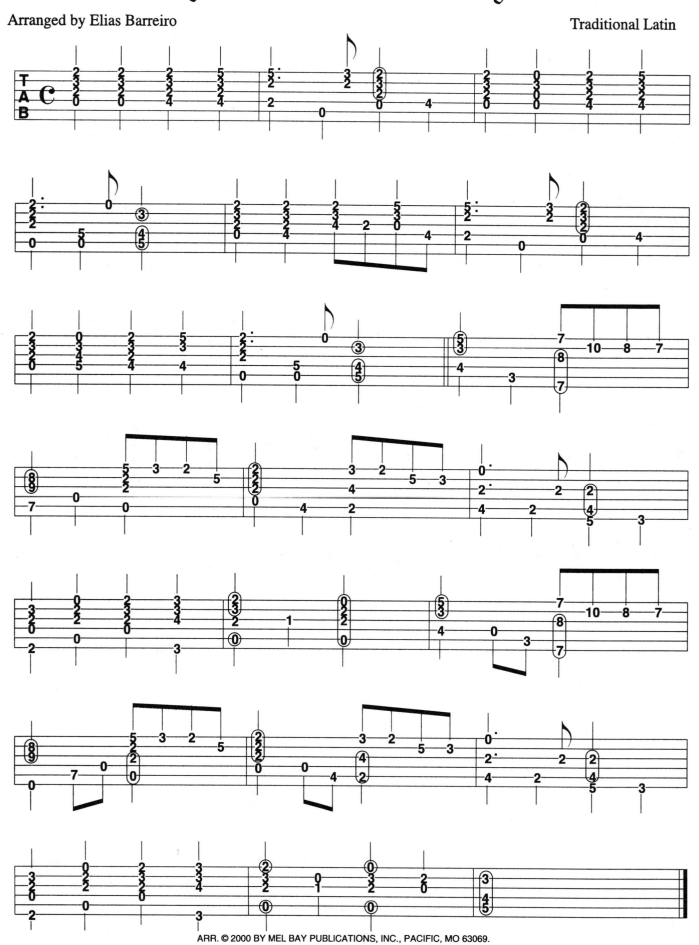

Going To Bethlehem
(Vamos a Belén)

Arranged by Elias Barreiro

Traditional Chilean

The First Nowell

Arranged by Elias Barreiro

Traditional English

⑥ = D

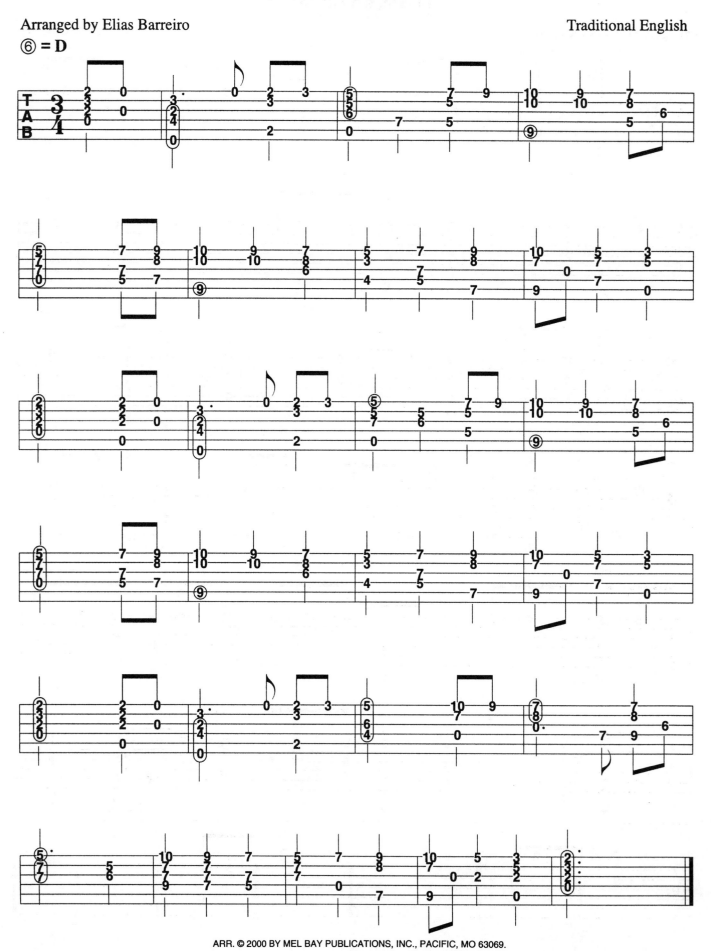

Coventry Carol

Arranged by Elias Barreiro

Traditional English

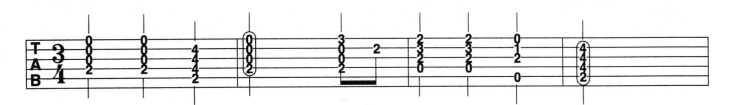

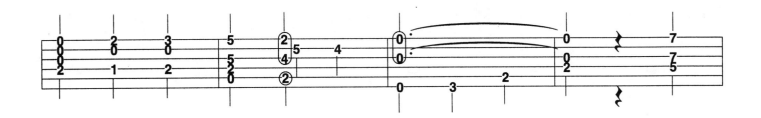

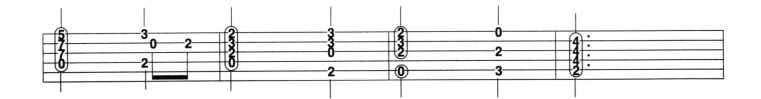

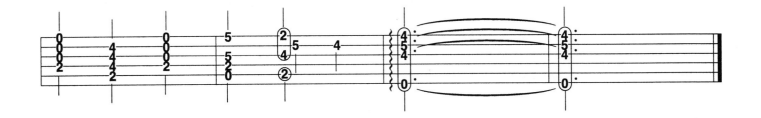

Cántico

Arranged by Elias Barreiro

Traditional Venezuelan

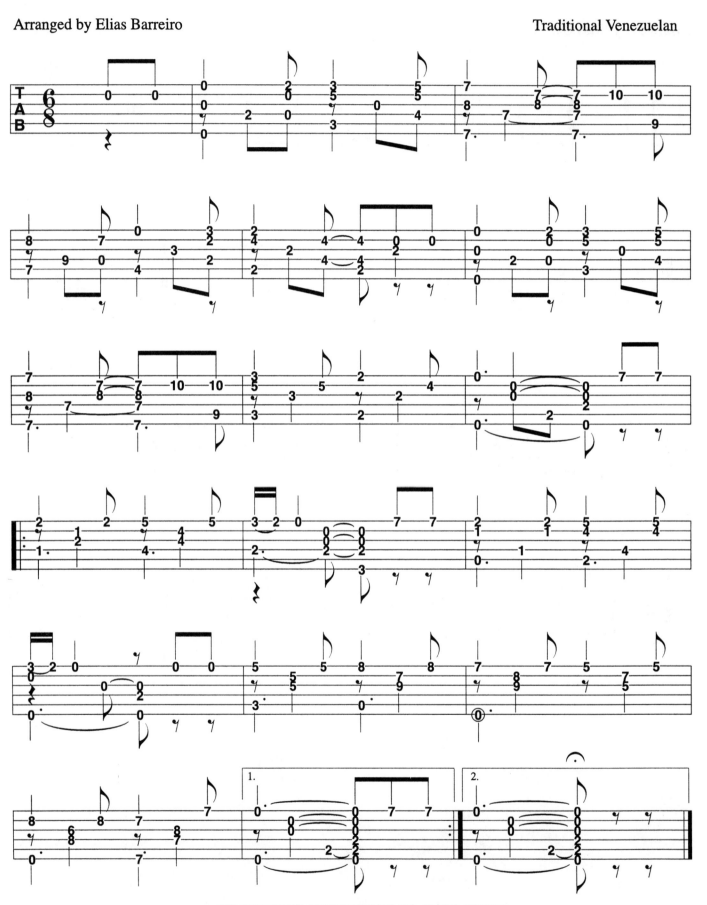

Silent Night, Holy Night
(Stille Nacht, Heilige Nacht)

Arranged by Elias Barreiro

Franz X. Gruber
(1787-1863)

Harm.
8va

O Come, All Ye Faithful
(Adestes Fideles)

Arranged by Elias Barreiro

Traditional Latin

The Three Ships

Arranged by Elias Barreiro

Traditional English

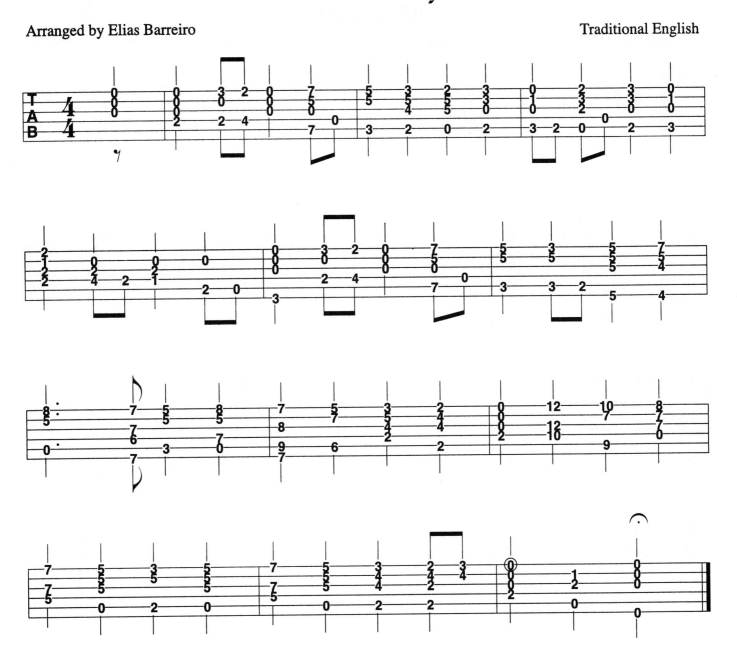

O Bethlehem
(Oi Betlehem)

Arranged by Elias Barreiro

Traditional Spanish (Vizcaya)

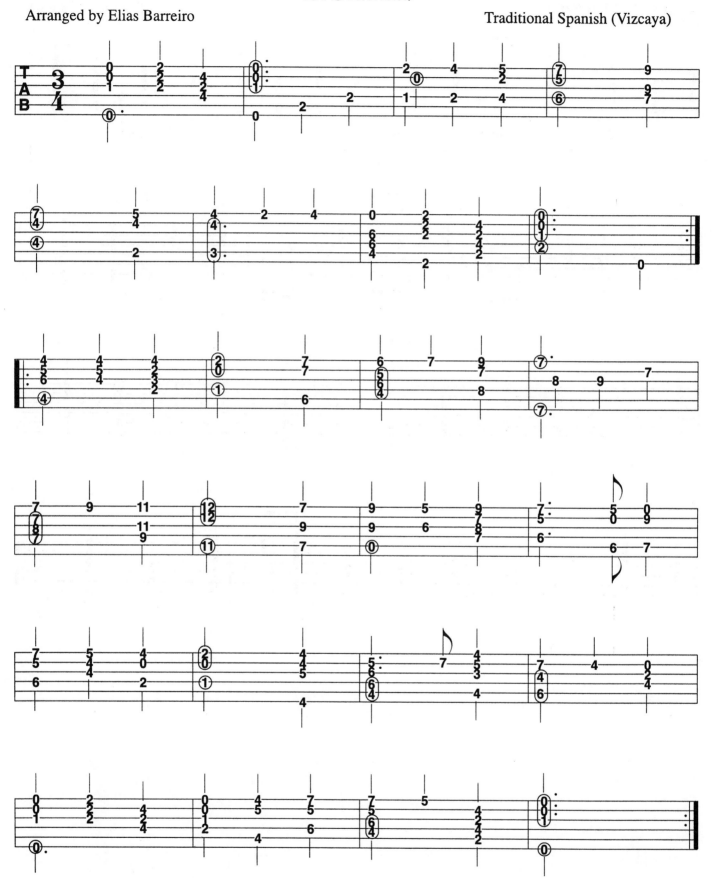

O Christmas Tree
(O Tannenbaum)

Arranged by Elias Barreiro

Traditional German

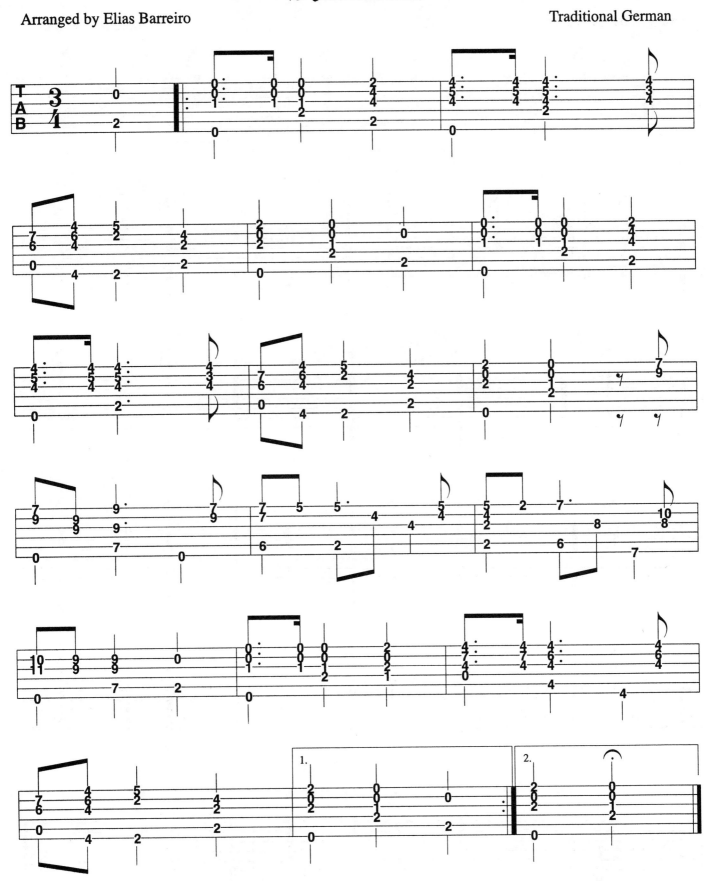

Good Christian Men, Rejoice

Arranged by Elias Barreiro

Traditional German

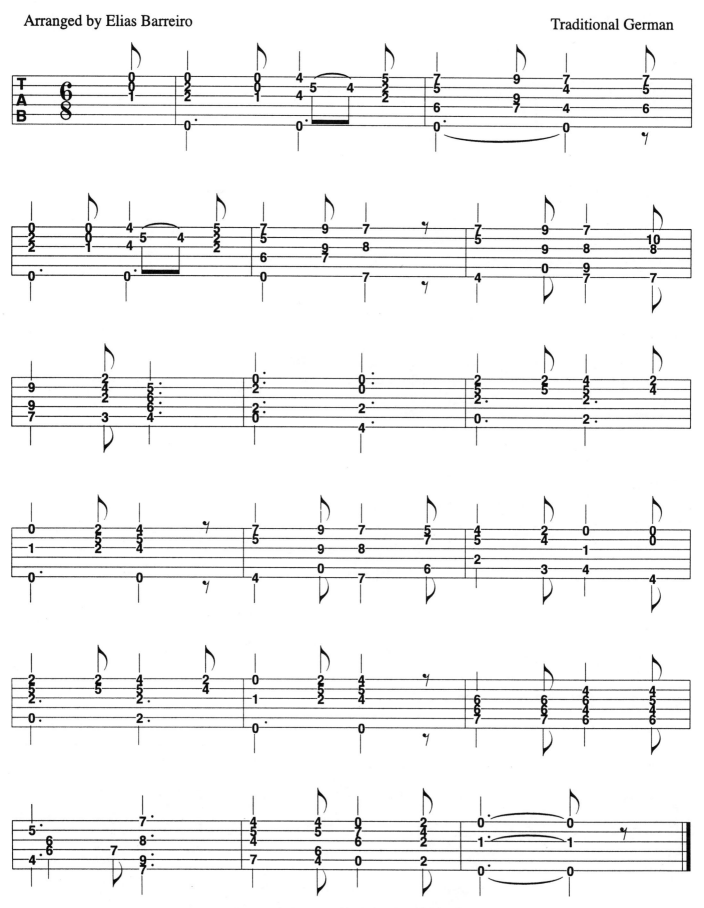

Hark! The Herald Angels Sing

Arranged by Elias Barreiro

Felix Mendelssonn
(1809-1847)

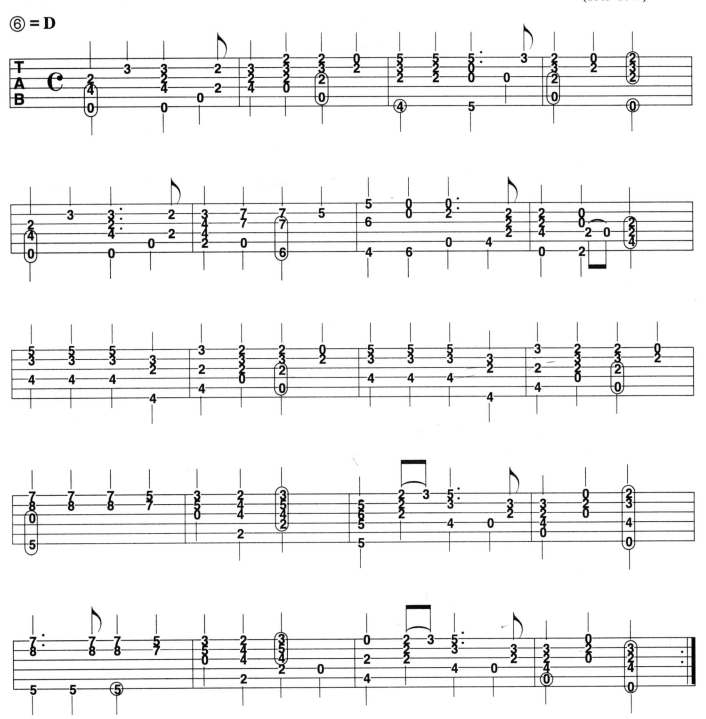

The Holy Child
(El Santo Niño)

Arranged by Elias Barreiro

Traditional Puerto Rican

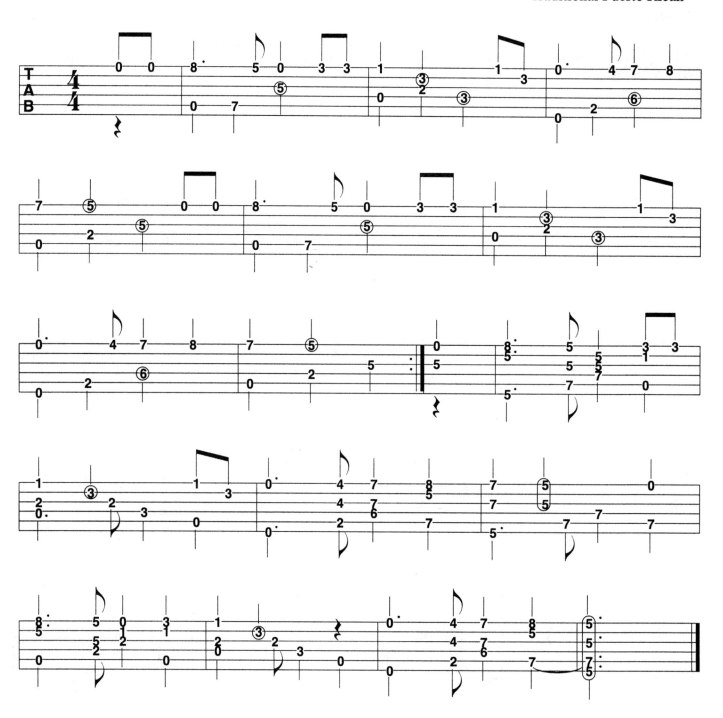

Masters in this Hall

Arranged by Elias Barreiro

Traditional French

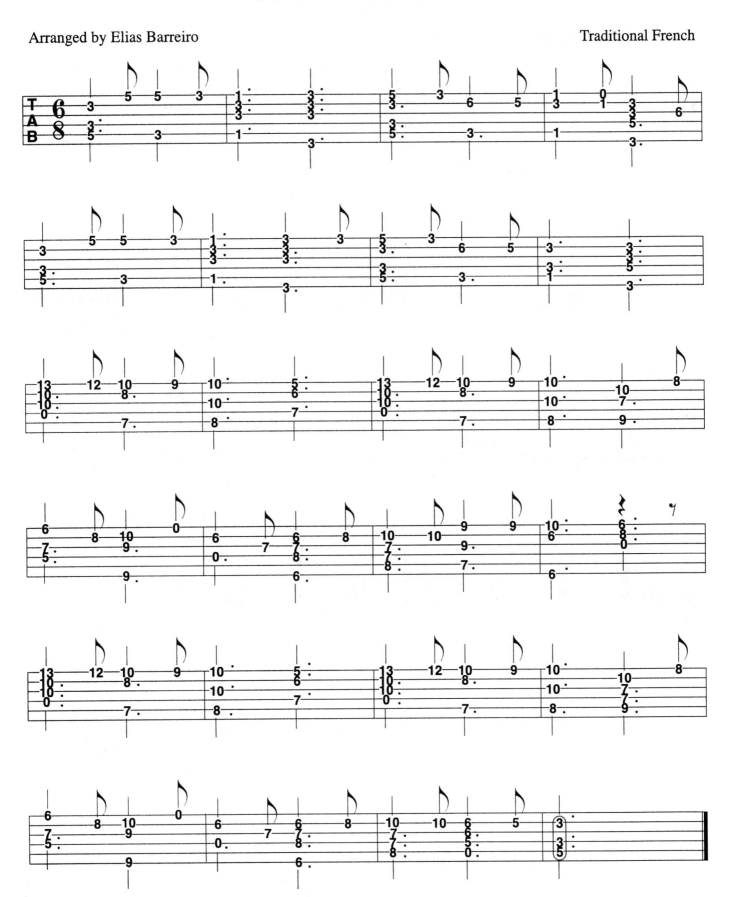

Good King Wenceslas

Arranged by Elias Barreiro

Traditional English

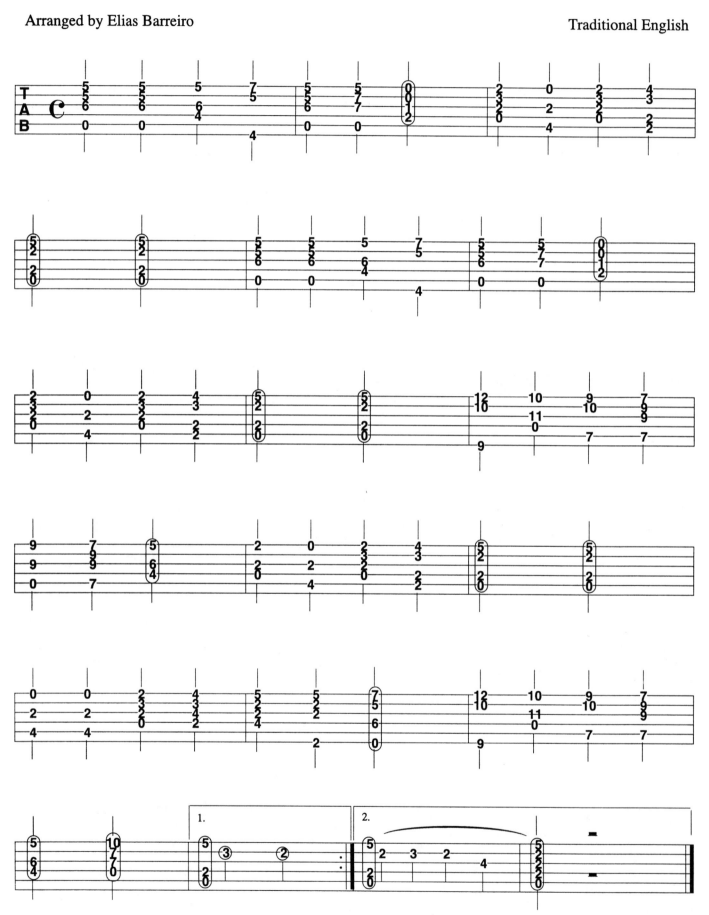

Jingle Bells

Arranged by Elias Barreiro

James Pierpont
(1822-1893)

Cantemos, Cantemos

Arranged by Elias Barreiro

Traditional Venezuelan

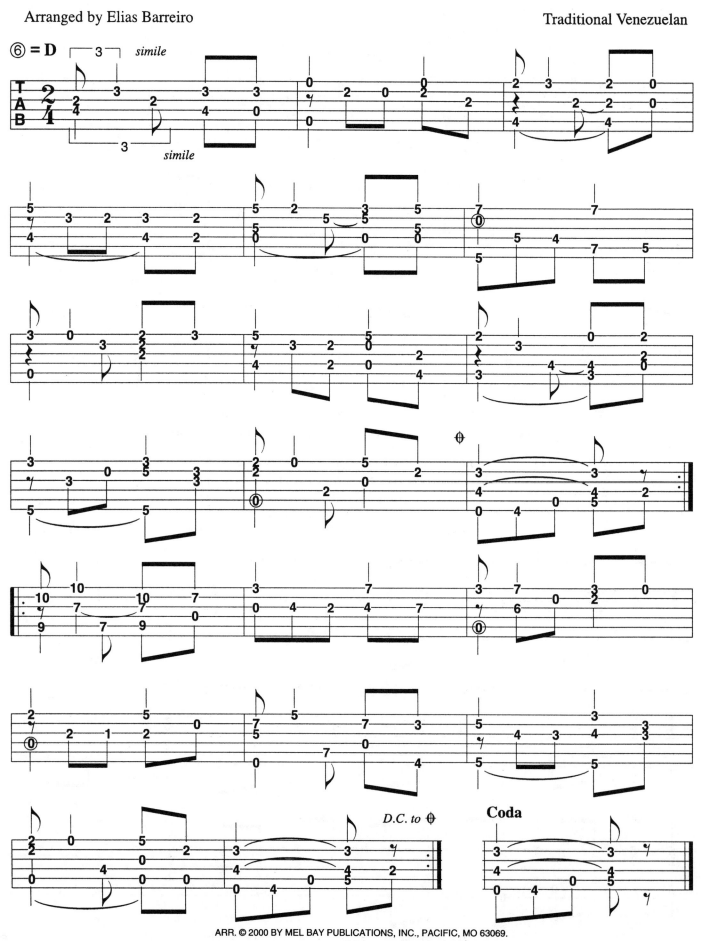

The Seven Joys of Mary

Arranged by Elias Barreiro

Traditional English

What Child Is This?

(Greensleeves)

Arranged by Elias Barreiro

Traditional English

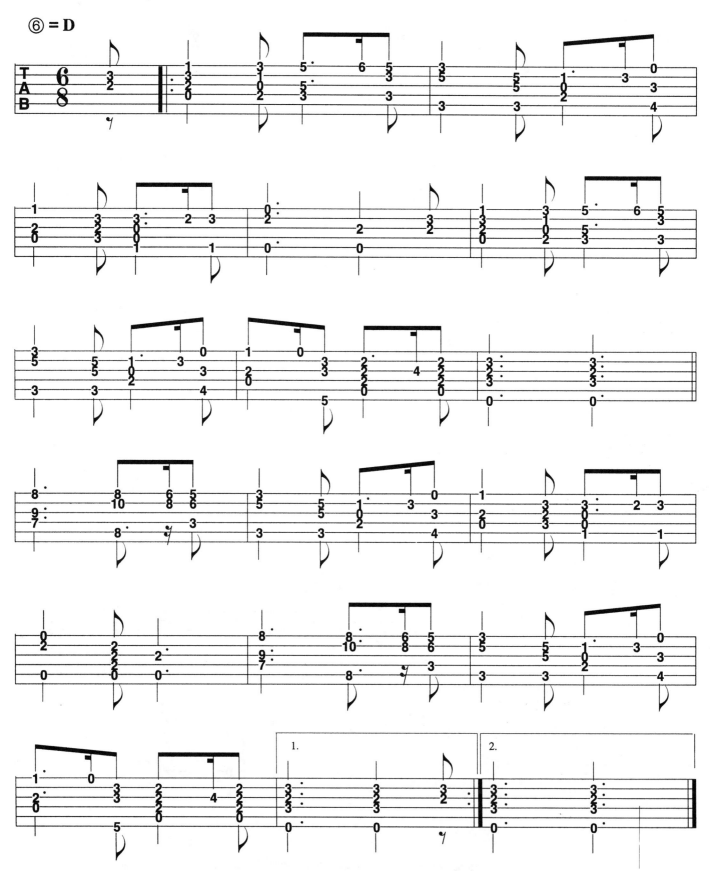

O Little Town of Bethlehem

Arranged by Elias Barreiro

Lewis H. Redner
(1831-1908)

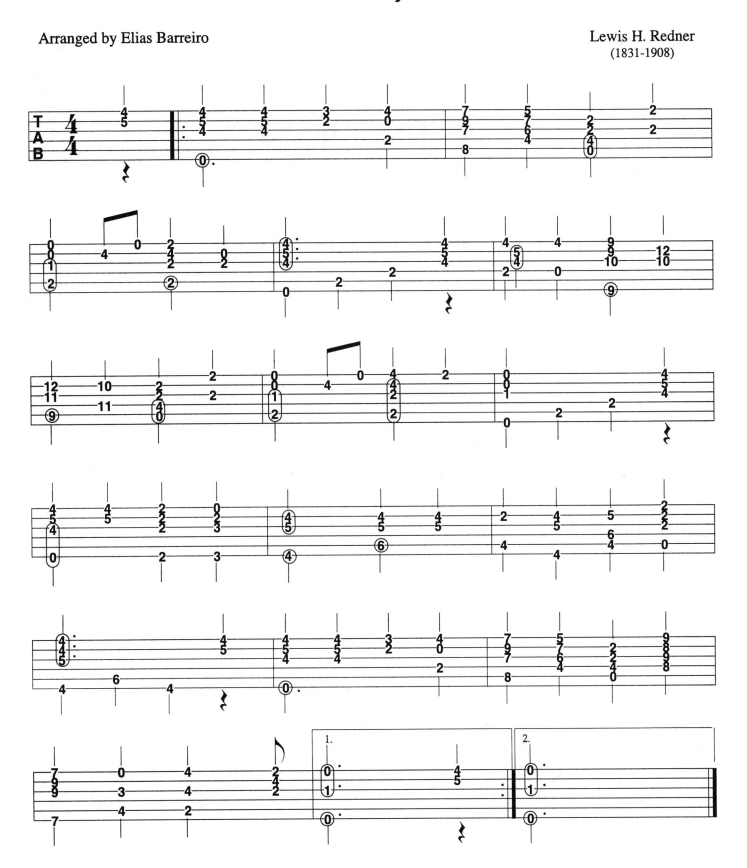

Deck the Halls

Arranged by Elias Barreiro

Traditional Welsh

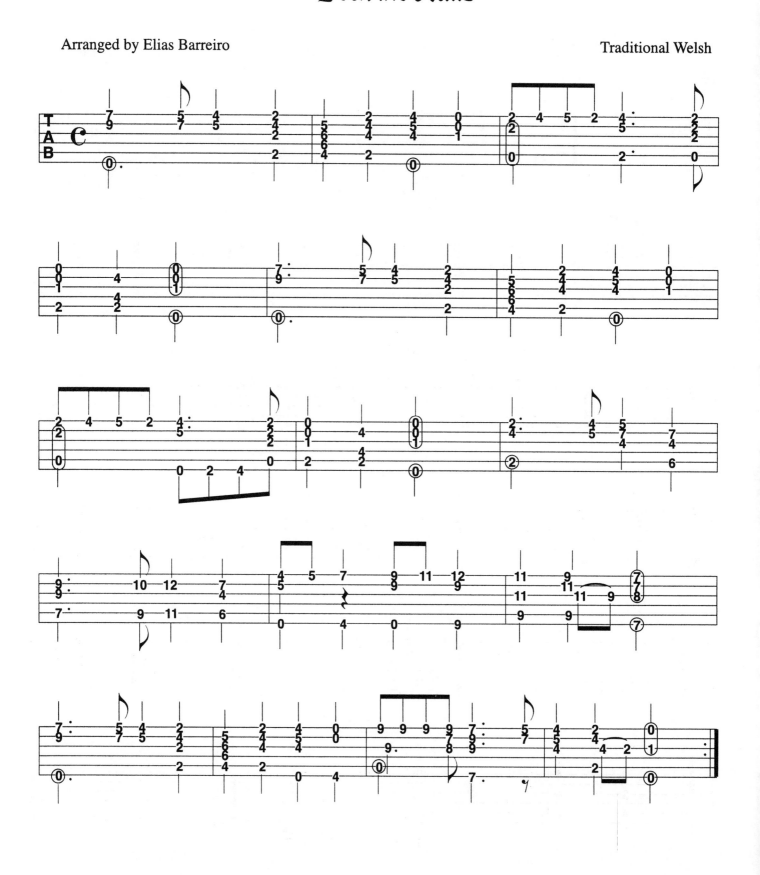

The Twelve Days of Christmas

Arranged by Elias Barreiro

Traditional English

Precioso Querube

Arranged by Elias Barreiro

Traditional Venezuelan

⑥ = D

We Wish You a Merry Christmas

Arranged by Elias Barreiro

Traditional English

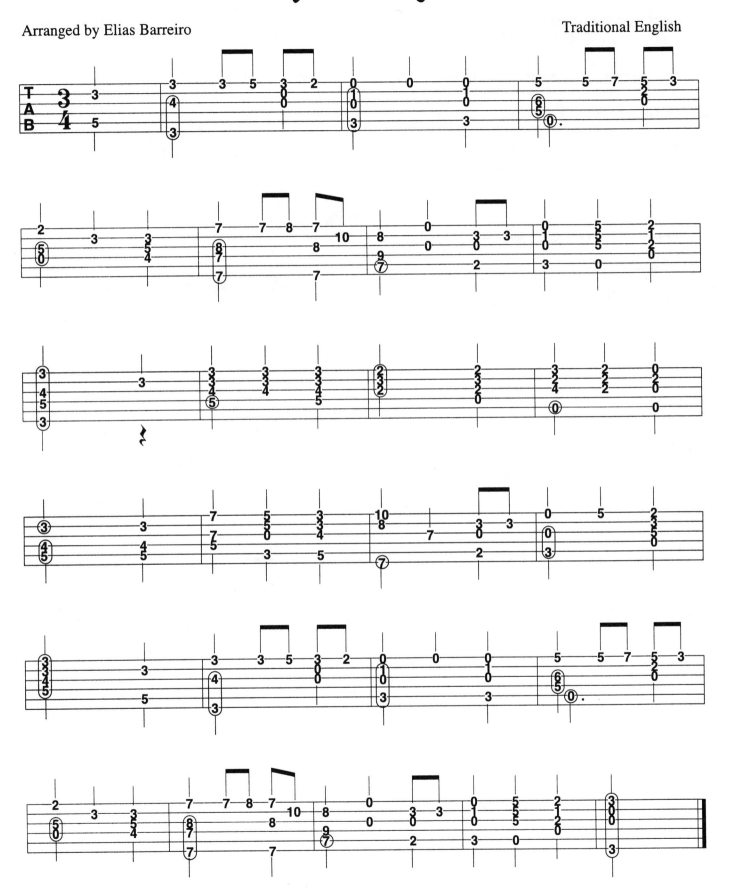

Jolly Old St. Nicholas

Arranged by Elias Barreiro

Traditional American

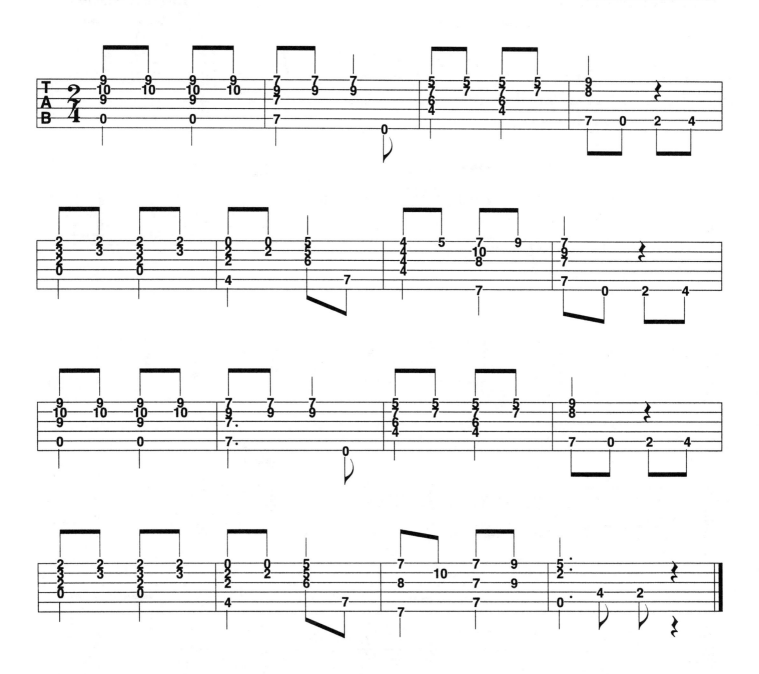

Away in a Manger

Arranged by Elias Barreiro

Traditional German
(Attributed to Martin Luther-1530)

Away in a Manger

Arranged by Elias Barreiro

Traditional English

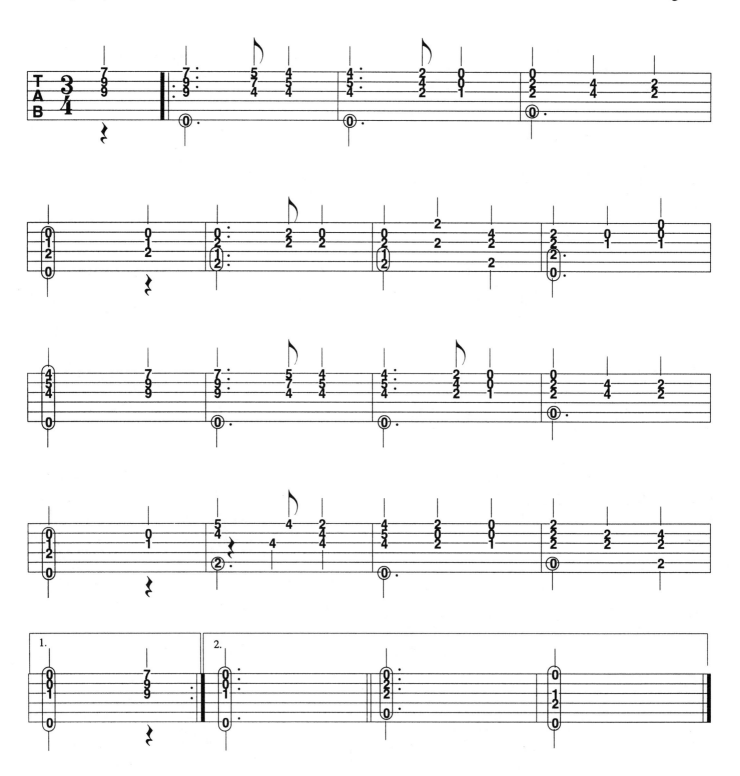

Away in a Manger

Arranged by Elias Barreiro

William J. Kirkpatrick
(USA 1838-1921)

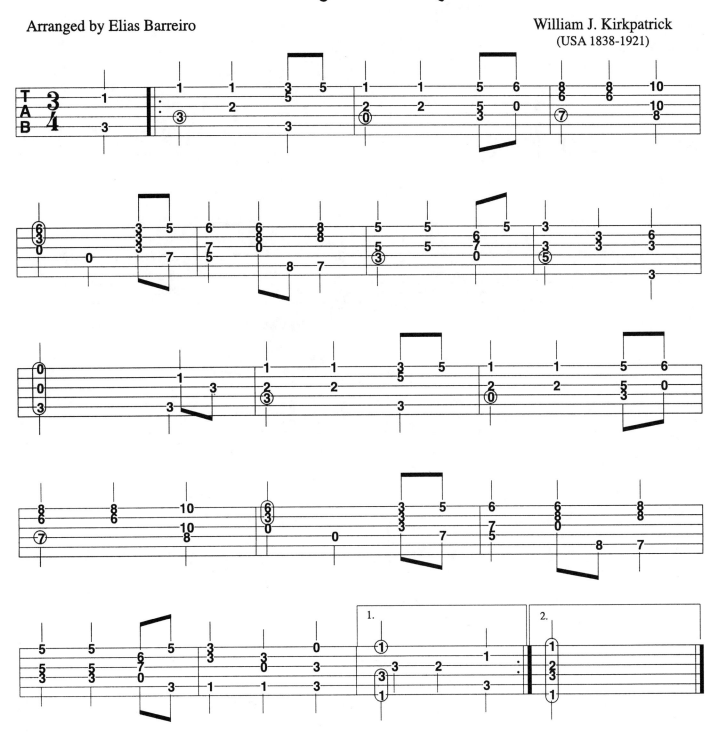

Away in a Manger

Arranged by Elias Barreiro

Traditional Basque

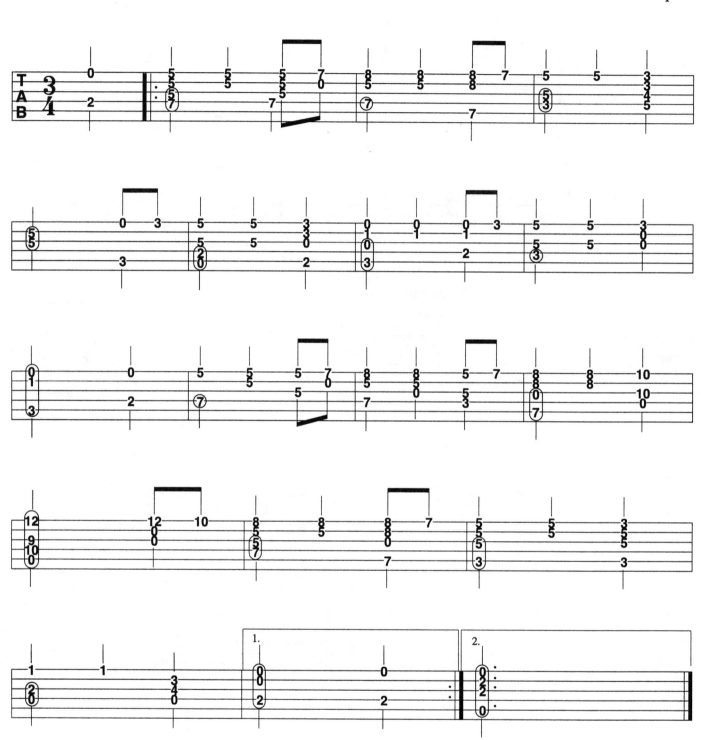

Joy to the World

Arranged by Elias Barreiro

George F. Handel
(1685-1759)

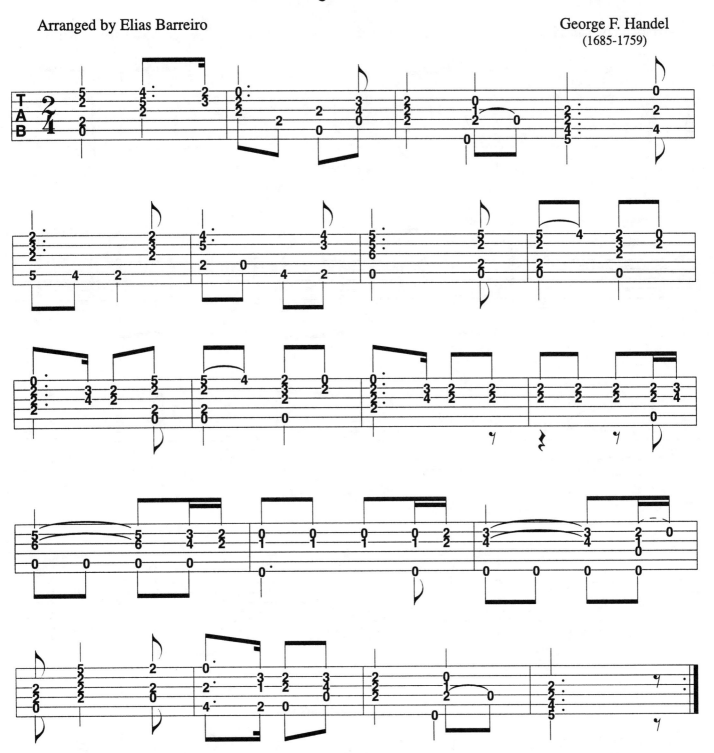

It Came Upon a Midnight Clear

Arranged by Elias Barreiro

Richard S. Willis
(1829-1900)

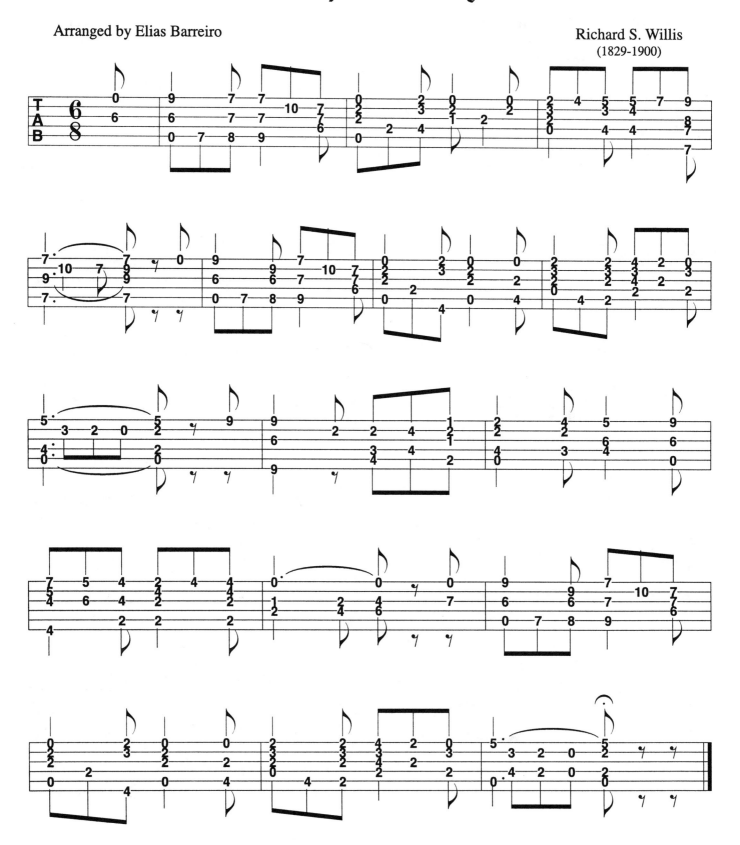

I Saw Three Ships

Arranged by Elias Barreiro

Traditional English

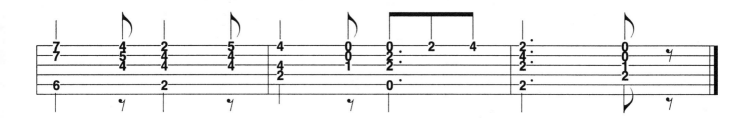

We Three Kings of Orient Are

Arranged by Elias Barreiro

John H. Hopkins
(1820-1891)

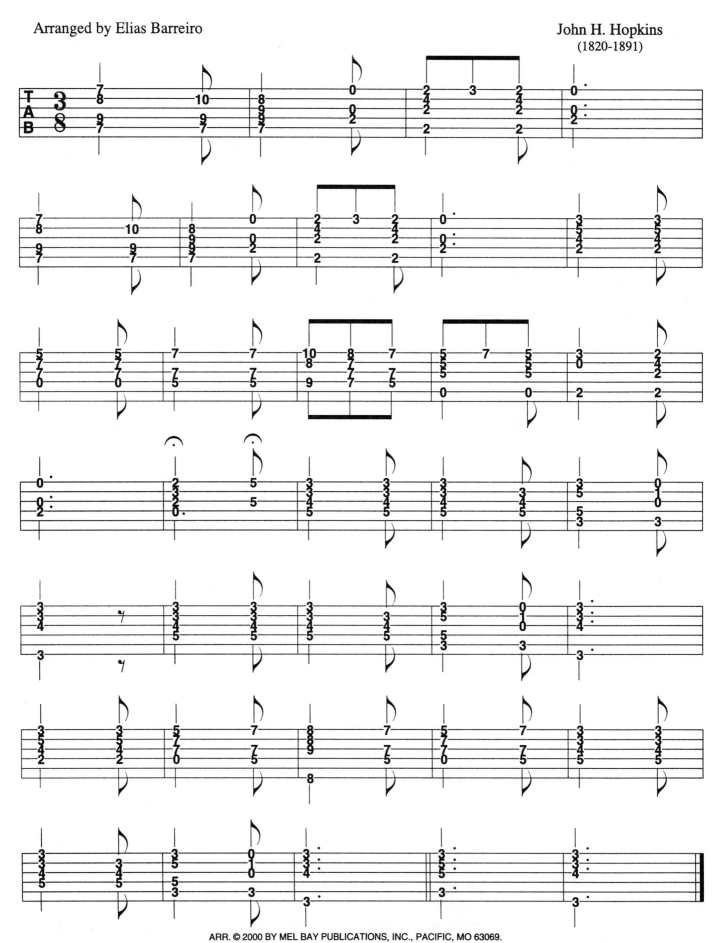

God Rest You Merry, Gentlemen

Arranged by Elias Barreiro

Traditional English

O Sanctissima

Arranged by Elias Barreiro

Traditional Sicilian